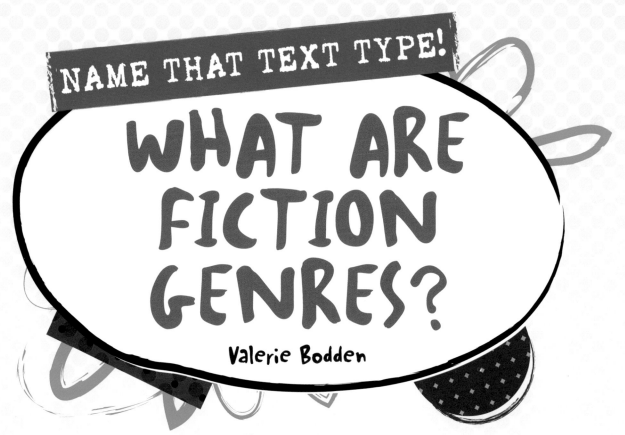

NAME THAT TEXT TYPE!

WHAT ARE FICTION GENRES?

Valerie Bodden

Lerner Publications Company • Minneapolis

For Mom and Dad, who never told me
not to tell stories

Lerner Publications Company
A division of Lerner Publishing Group, Inc.
241 First Avenue North
Minneapolis, MN 55401 USA

For reading levels and more information, look up this title at www.lernerbooks.com.

All fiction text examples copyright © by Lerner Publishing Group, Inc. All rights
reserved.

Main body text set in Avenir LT Pro 15/21. Typeface provided by Linotype AG.

Library of Congress Cataloging-in-Publication Data

Bodden, Valerie.
    What are fiction genres? / by Valerie Bodden.
       p.   cm. — (Name that text type!)
    Includes index.
    ISBN 978–1–4677–3664–0 (lib. bdg. : alk. paper)
    ISBN 978–1–4677–4698–4 (eBook)
    1. Fiction genres—Juvenile literature. I. Title.
  PN3427.B63 2015
  808.3—dc23   2013037677

Manufactured in the United States of America
1 – BP – 7/15/14

Contents

Has this happened to you? You start reading a book. Soon you forget where you are. You feel as though you are on a ship. Or you are fighting a dragon. Maybe you are solving a mystery.

That's the great thing about fiction. It takes you into other worlds. It lets you meet other people.

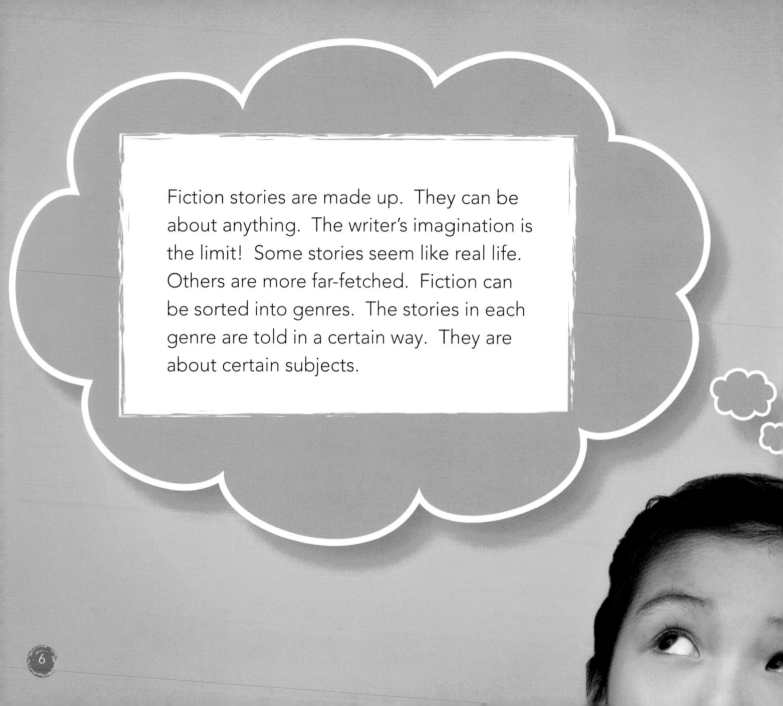

Fiction stories are made up. They can be about anything. The writer's imagination is the limit! Some stories seem like real life. Others are more far-fetched. Fiction can be sorted into genres. The stories in each genre are told in a certain way. They are about certain subjects.

TELLING THE STORY

All fiction stories have characters, settings, and plots. Characters are the people in the story. Characters can be animals too. They can even be other beings. Many stories have one main character. The story is mostly about this character. Stories can have good or bad characters. Bad characters cause problems for the main character.

The setting is where and when a story happens. Stories can happen anytime. They can be set in the past. Or they can take place in the present. Some stories are set in the future.

Stories can happen anywhere too. Settings can be real places. Or a setting can be made up. A story might take place at a school. Or it might be set on a train. A story can even take place on another planet!

What happens in a story is called the plot. All stories have a beginning, a middle, and an end. A story might start with a problem. The middle of the story tells more about the problem. It shows how the problem affects the main character.

At the story's climax, the character must face the problem. This is the most exciting part of the story. It is when the hero fights the dragon. It might be when the kid stands up to the bully. The end of the story tells what happens after the climax. Sometimes the characters live happily ever after. Other times they don't.

Some stories have pictures. The pictures help tell the story. They show how characters feel. Pictures let you see the setting. They help you imagine the plot. They can give you clues about what will happen next.

IN THE REAL WORLD

Different genres use different kinds of characters, settings, and plots. Realistic fiction is set in the present. Its characters are made up. But they seem like real people. The characters face real-life problems. They might have trouble in school. Or they might argue with friends.

Look for the real-life problems in this story:

Meg sat at the back of the bus. She hoped no one would see her. Then maybe the other girls wouldn't tease her. But of course they saw her. And of course they teased her. Just because she wore old shoes. Just because her jacket was too small. Could she help it that her dad had lost his job?

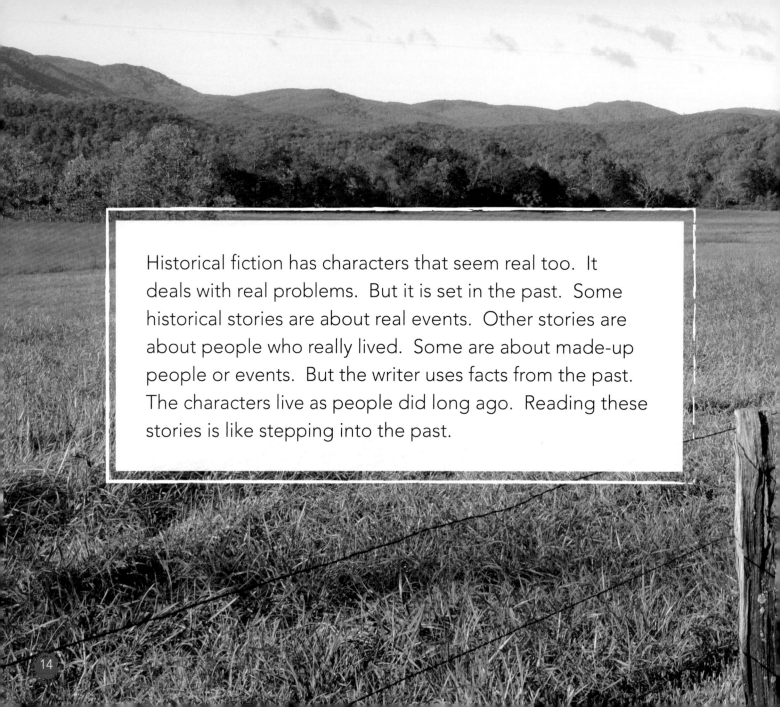

Historical fiction has characters that seem real too. It deals with real problems. But it is set in the past. Some historical stories are about real events. Other stories are about people who really lived. Some are about made-up people or events. But the writer uses facts from the past. The characters live as people did long ago. Reading these stories is like stepping into the past.

Would you like to step into this story?

Anne sat in the wagon. She watched the horses' tails swish. She could tell the horses were tired. Anne was tired too. Her body was sore. Dust covered her dress. Her family had been riding in the wagon for days. But it would take weeks to reach their new home in the West.

GET YOUR HEART PUMPING

Some stories make your heart pound. You keep reading to find out what happens next. You can tell a mystery by its plot. A mystery starts with a puzzle. Something might be missing. Or someone found something strange. The main character looks for clues. She tries to solve the mystery. Readers try to solve the mystery too. Sometimes they solve it before the main character does.

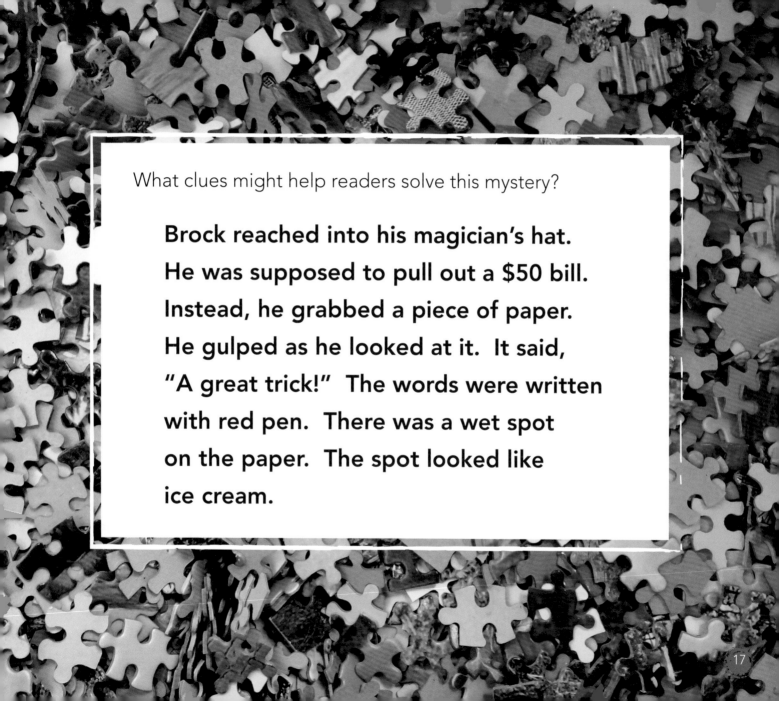

What clues might help readers solve this mystery?

Brock reached into his magician's hat.
He was supposed to pull out a $50 bill.
Instead, he grabbed a piece of paper.
He gulped as he looked at it. It said,
"A great trick!" The words were written
with red pen. There was a wet spot
on the paper. The spot looked like
ice cream.

An adventure story is all about action. These stories move fast. The main character has one adventure after another. He might be trying to survive in the wild. Or she might need to save someone from an enemy. The main character might have close calls. But he usually escapes just in time.

What kind of adventure might have led to this escape?

Zac ran to the tree. He looked around. The growling dog was getting close. In a few seconds, it would bite him. Zac yelled for help. But there was no one around. Zac grabbed a tree branch. He pulled his feet up. The dog jumped for him. It got his shoelaces, but Zac pulled free. He was safe—for now!

The purpose of a scary story is simple: to scare you. The bad character is often a monster. It might be a ghost or a vampire. The monster might chase the main character. Or it might try to hurt people. The main character has to beat the monster. You feel scared as you read. You can tell something bad will happen.

What clues tell you this is a scary story?

A crash shook the house. Mai sat up in bed. She looked around wildly. It was just a storm. But then she heard something else: a scratching sound. It was coming from the closet. Mai stared through the dark. But she couldn't see anything. Suddenly, lightning lit the room. Mai screamed. The closet door was opening.

Some stories take place in other worlds. These worlds are not like anything we know. Science fiction stories use science to create a new world. Writers imagine what science could make possible. Their stories might have machines or robots. They might take place on another planet. Or they can be set in the future.

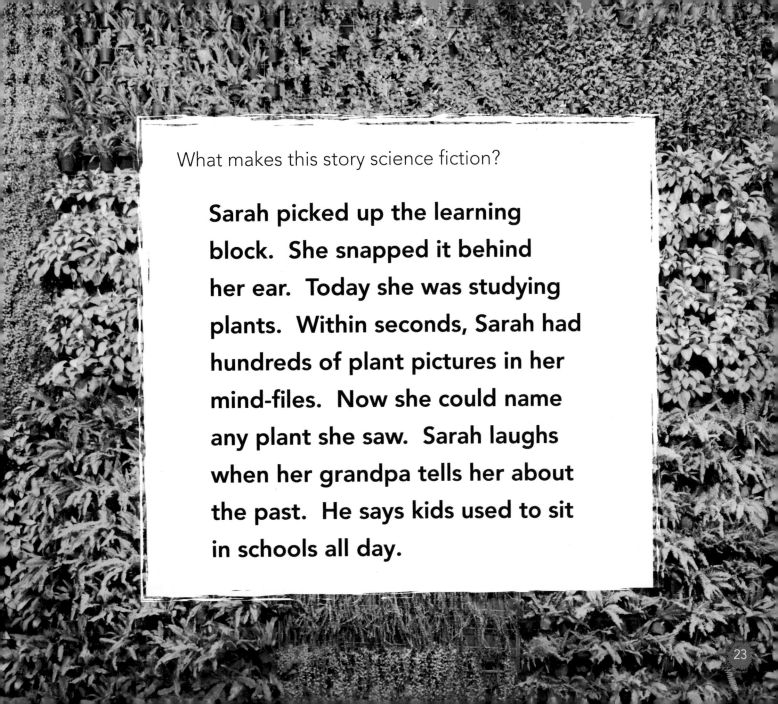

What makes this story science fiction?

Sarah picked up the learning block. She snapped it behind her ear. Today she was studying plants. Within seconds, Sarah had hundreds of plant pictures in her mind-files. Now she could name any plant she saw. Sarah laughs when her grandpa tells her about the past. He says kids used to sit in schools all day.

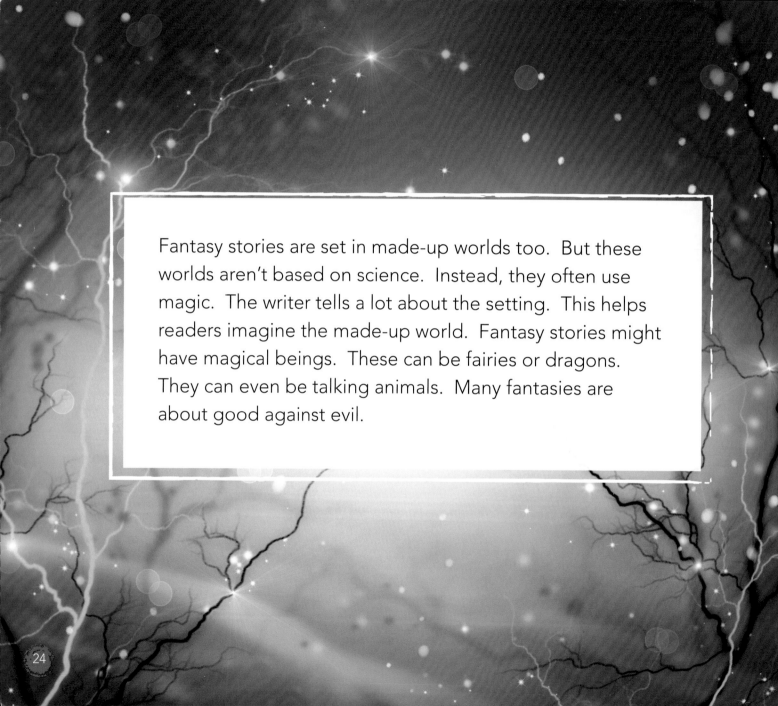

Fantasy stories are set in made-up worlds too. But these worlds aren't based on science. Instead, they often use magic. The writer tells a lot about the setting. This helps readers imagine the made-up world. Fantasy stories might have magical beings. These can be fairies or dragons. They can even be talking animals. Many fantasies are about good against evil.

Try to picture this world:

The night-sun gave off a soft blue light. The light shone on hundreds of unicorns. The unicorns had gathered at the One Field. Some stood in groups. They talked softly. Others ate the sweet grass. Many looked around nervously. They knew the Dark Herd was getting closer.

MIXING IT UP

Not all stories fit into one genre. Some writers use ideas from more than one genre in the same story. A fantasy might have adventures. Or a historical story might include a mystery.

finding day's bottom

CANDICE RANSOM

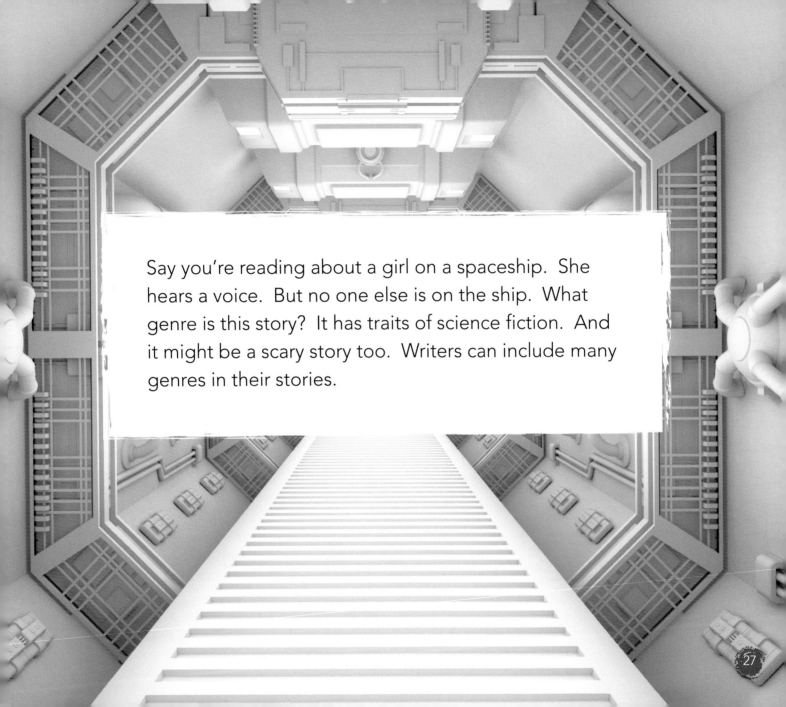

Say you're reading about a girl on a spaceship. She hears a voice. But no one else is on the ship. What genre is this story? It has traits of science fiction. And it might be a scary story too. Writers can include many genres in their stories.

What genres do you like best? Do you love to be scared?
Maybe you like stories about kids like you. The more you
read, the more you'll learn what kinds of books you like.
So grab a scary story. Or pick up some realistic fiction.
You will find things you never imagined!

Now You Do It

1. Fiction stories need characters, setting, and plot. Write a paragraph about a character you could use in a story. What does he or she look like? What does the character like to do? Then write a paragraph about the setting. Is it a school? Is it an old castle? Next, think about what could happen to your character in that setting. Is a monster after her? Did he get in trouble? Write a paragraph about the plot.

2. Realistic and historical fiction take place in the real world. Write a paragraph about a real-world setting. It could be your bedroom. Maybe it is the park down the street. Try to make readers feel as though they are there with you. What would they see and hear? Are there any smells?

3. You are sitting in your classroom. Suddenly you hear a scream in the hallway. But when you go to the door, no one is there. Write what happens next. You can make it a mystery. Write about the clues you find. Or you can make it a scary story. Is there a monster on the loose?

4. Imagine a world that is different from anything you have ever seen. Where is it? When is it? Who lives there? Write about what this strange world is like.

Glossary

character: a person (or creature) in a story

climax: the most exciting or important part of a story

fantasy: a story about a made-up world, often with magical beings

fiction: stories that are made up

future: a time that has not happened yet

genre: a type of story. A story's genre is based on how the story is told and what it is about.

historical: having to do with the past

mystery: a story in which a character has to solve a crime or other strange event

plot: what happens in a story

realistic: based on real life or seeming like real life

science fiction: a story about science, set in the future or on another planet

setting: where and when a story takes place

Further Information

Knudsen, Shannon. *I'm a Fire Breather! Meet a Dragon.* Minneapolis: Millbrook Press, 2015. Want to learn about monsters in fiction stories? Follow Alice the dragon on an adventure as she teaches you all about dragons!

Owings, Lisa. *What Are Legends, Folktales, and Other Classic Stories?* Minneapolis: Lerner Publications, 2015. Learn about legends, myths, folktales, fables, and fairy tales, and find out how these genres are different from other kinds of writing.

PBS Kids: Writers Contest
http://pbskids.org/writerscontest
Do you have a story to tell? Submit your best story and artwork to this writing contest. If you win, you'll get a prize!

Spinelli, Eileen. *The Best Story.* New York: Dial Books for Young Readers, 2008. The library is having a contest for the best story, and the main character in this book wants to win! Find out how she decides what kind of story will be the best.

Stone Soup
http://www.stonesoup.com
This creative writing magazine is written and illustrated by kids aged eight to thirteen. Read stories and poems by other kids and submit your own work!

Expand learning beyond the printed book. Download free, complementary educational resources for this book from our website, www.lernerresource.com.

Index

Photo Acknowledgments

The images in this book are used with the permission of: © Togataki/Shutterstock.com, pp. 2, 30, 31, 32; © kurt/Shutterstock.com, p. 4; © Pakhnyushcha/Shutterstock.com, p. 5; © Patrick Foto/Shutterstock.com, p. 6; © Lerner Publishing Group, Inc., pp. 7 (all), 10, 11, 12, 20, 26; © Sigapo/Shutterstock.com, p. 8; © MaxyM/Shutterstock.com, p. 13; © Neta Degany/Thinkstock, p. 14; © Frontpage/Shutterstock.com, p. 15; © Butterfly Hunter/Shutterstock.com, p. 16; © Outlandish/Shutterstock.com, p. 17; © andreiuc88/Shutterstock.com, p. 18; © Reddogs/Shutterstock.com, p. 19; © Piotr Krzeslak/Shutterstock.com, p. 21; © VikaSuh/Bigstock.com, p. 22; © Adisa/Shutterstock.com, p. 23; © Subbotina Anna/Shutterstock.com, p. 24; © Calmando/Shutterstock.com, p. 25; © F. Schmidt/Shutterstock.com, p. 27; © jannoon028/Shutterstock.com, p. 28; © Photoraidz/Shutterstock.com, p. 29.

Front cover: © Lerner Publishing Group, Inc. (iPad inset and bottom illustration); © robert_s/Shutterstock.com (iPad).